Six Themes
Everyone Should Know

# The Bible

Barry Ensign-George

Geneva
Press

*Cover designer: Rebecca Kueber*

**Library of Congress Cataloging-in-Publication Data**

Names: Ensign-George, Barry A., author.
Title: Six themes in the Bible everyone should know / Barry Ensign-George.
Description: First [edition]. | Louisville, KY : Geneva Press, 2019. |
   Series: Six themes everyone should know series
Identifiers: LCCN 2018036028 (print) | LCCN 2018052647 (ebook) | ISBN
   9781611649246 (ebook) | ISBN 9781571532374 (pbk.)
Subjects: LCSH: Bible--Theology--Textbooks.
Classification: LCC BS543 (ebook) | LCC BS543 .E57 2019 (print) | DDC
   220.6--dc23
LC record available at https://lccn.loc.gov/2018036028

Most Geneva Press books are available at special quantity discounts when purchased in bulk by corporations, organizations, and special-interest groups. For more information, please e-mail SpecialSales@GenevaPress.com.

# Contents

## *Six Themes Everyone Should Know* series

*The Bible,* by Barry Ensign-George

*Genesis,* by W. Eugene March

*Matthew,* by James E. Davison

*Luke,* by John T. Carroll

*1 and 2 Timothy,* by Thomas G. Long

# Introduction to the
## *Six Themes Everyone Should Know* series

The *Six Themes Everyone Should Know* series focuses on the study of Scripture. Bible study is vital to the lives of churches. Churches need ways of studying Scripture that can fit a variety of contexts and group needs. *Six Themes Everyone Should Know* studies offer a central feature of church adult educational programs. Their flexibility and accessibility make it possible to have short-term studies that introduce biblical books and their main themes.

*Six Themes Everyone Should Know* consists of six chapters that introduce major biblical themes. At the core of each chapter is an introduction and three major sections. These sections relate to key dimensions of Bible study. These sections ask:

- What does this biblical theme mean?
- What is the meaning of this biblical theme for the life of faith?
- What does this biblical theme mean for the church at this point in history for action?

This format presents a compact and accessible way for people in various educational settings to gain knowledge about major themes in the biblical books; to experience the impact of what Scripture means for Christian devotion to God; and to consider ways Scripture can lead to new directions for the church in action.

# Introduction to *The Bible*

This first study in the *Six Themes Everyone Should Know* series takes a wide-angle look at the Bible rather than focusing on a specific biblical book as the other studies do. Here the great arc of God's mission is traced "From the Garden to the Garden City." Barry Ensign-George looks at six themes that begin in the early chapters of Genesis, span the pages of Scripture, and end with the glorious vision of the book of Revelation—of the new Jerusalem, the city of the redeemed of God.

This study is important for discussing basic biblical frameworks. Within Scripture, echoes of early themes are picked up and heard, leading to deeper appreciations of the biblical message.

The *Six Themes Everyone Should Know* studies introduce major themes found in biblical books. These themes will be explored in themselves, for their values in the life of faith, and what they direct us toward in terms of the church's life and action in the world. To see these themes in relation to the backdrops offered in *Six Themes in the Bible Everyone Should Know* will enliven these biblical studies with wider perspectives for deeper understandings and personal appropriation.

We are pleased to present this introduction and to welcome you to *Six Themes in The Bible Everyone Should Know*.

# Preface

When we study the Bible we usually find ourselves focusing on small units of the whole: a single book, a specific chapter, or a few verses. We dive deep, seeking to understand and to learn these smaller units, looking for what they have to teach us. This is a good way to approach Scripture, and it has significant rewards.

Less often do we consider the sweep of the Bible from Genesis to Revelation. Some are inclined to claim that there is no grand sweep—only the smaller units matter. But the Bible is constructed more carefully than that. It is put together in ways that are complex, yes, but not random.

This study invites you to consider the grand sweep. The chapters of this study will look at six themes that are launched in Genesis 1—11 and then thread across the Bible, in most cases finding their final landing point in Revelation.

The grand sweep of the Bible could be explored by beginning from other starting points. Chapter 6 explores one of them: it considers Jesus Christ in the Gospel of John, who was, the Gospel tells us, there "In the beginning . . ." (John 1:1) and who goes ahead to God's presence where "In my Father's house there are many dwelling places" (John 14:2). One could start in other places as well, illuminating the grand sweep of the Bible along other lines. My hope for these six chapters is that the ideas explored here will be valuable in helping you make your own explorations of Scripture.

These studies are offered in part as helpers. I hope you will find them to be helpful in finding still other aspects of Scripture over its long stretch. That has been my experience over the last several years as I have worked with the material that makes up the content of the studies. I would read or hear someone's insight into Genesis chapters 1–11, or an insight into Revelation's account of the new Jerusalem, and suddenly I would begin hearing resonances, unexpected echoes of that insight in other places in Scripture. Or, to use a slightly different image, an insight that I read or heard would begin to illuminate other parts of Scripture in ways that I had never seen before. I would find connections being made where I hadn't seen them before nor anticipated them. I hope that you will have similar experiences as you work through these studies.

I am grateful to those whose insights have set off resonances for me. The footnotes in the study are a small way of saying a partial "thank you!" But there have been others along the way to whom I am deeply grateful. Among them are the members of the North-Central group of the Pastor-Theologian program of the Center of Theological Inquiry, the Exploring the Faith Class at Anchorage Presbyterian Church, Duane Hix, my colleagues in the Office of Theology and Worship, friends who have been part of the Core Cluster of the Re-Forming Ministry Program, and many others.

Barry Ensign-George

*The Garden of Eden, at the Bible's beginning, is also
in its end, the new Jerusalem.*

## Chapter 1

# The Great Arc of Creation: From Garden to Garden City

## Scripture
**Genesis 2:4–15**   God's work of creation begins, making a place for first communion with God and others.

**Revelation 21:9–14; 22:1–5**   God's work of creation will come to its goal where there will be full communion with God and others.

## Prayer
Gracious and loving God, source of life, as we turn to your word draw us deeper into communion with you, that we might be more fully in communion with all those who love and follow you. Empower us to be effective and faithful agents of your work to gather all into the future full communion with you and one another. This we ask in the name of our Savior, Jesus Christ. Amen.

## Introduction
This chapter is our first step in recognizing themes that stretch across the Bible. There are themes running across Scripture because the books of the Bible have a common set of primary characters: God, and the creation that God engages. The aim of this chapter and the five that follow is to recognize the larger thematic and narrative architecture of the Bible. This larger architecture is the work of editors who collected and shaped the writings that were gathered together and ordered in the canon of Scripture.

1

The stories of the Garden of Eden at the beginning of the Bible, and of the new Jerusalem at the end are both ways of thinking about and exploring reality. They are a bit like Jesus' parables. The stories of Eden and new Jerusalem explore what reality is, focusing on the relationship of God to us and the reality in which we live. They invite us to think about reality in and through stories. The chapters of this study seek to guide us in thinking about reality, about our world and the cosmos through the story and stories the Bible tells, a particular way the Bible thinks about our world and about life.

This chapter focuses on the connection between the beginning and ending of the Bible; between the Garden of Eden at the beginning of the book of Genesis and the garden city, the new Jerusalem at the end of the book of Revelation. The two are deeply connected, and in that connection, there is a rich theology. The connection is rooted in God's good purposes, the mission of God that shapes the movement from beginning to end. The connection offers us assurance that God knows, loves, and values us and all creatures around us. Life is not merely random, but God has a purpose, and we are invited to be agents of God's purpose—as individuals and as the church.

## A Basic Theme: The Garden of Eden and the Garden City

"In my beginning is my end," poet T.S. Eliot wrote, concluding the poem with "In my end is my beginning."[1] Eliot's insight is deeply biblical. The Garden of Eden, at the Bible's beginning, is also in its end, the new Jerusalem. Elements of Scripture's end are there already in the beginning, the Garden of Eden.

The Garden of Eden is present in the new Jerusalem in two particularly important features: tree and water.

There are many trees in Eden, "pleasant to the sight and good for food." (It's interesting that beauty comes first. Humans do not live by fruit alone!) "In the midst" of the garden are two special trees: the tree of life, and the fateful tree of the knowledge of good and evil (Genesis 2:9). Here, at the beginning of creation's story, the fruit of these special trees is dangerous, with effects the two humans cannot envision. The tree of life is growing in the middle

1. T.S. Eliot, "East Coker," in T.S. Eliot, *Collected Poems 1909-1962* (London: Faber and Faber Limited, 1974), 196–204.

of the new Jerusalem as well, but now its fruit produces fullness of life: "On either side of the river is the tree of life with its twelve kinds of fruit" (Revelation 22:2b).

There is flowing water in both places. Genesis 2:10–14 tells of a river flowing out of the garden, then dividing into four great rivers: the Pishon, Gihon, Tigris, and Euphrates. The latter two are well known. The former two are obscure. That obscurity serves to make the point. The list of rivers and regions is meant to suggest the world: the world is irrigated by the life-giving waters that flow out of the Garden of Eden. The river that brings life to all is also there in the new Jerusalem: "Then the angel showed me the river of the water of life, bright as crystal, flowing from the throne of God and of the Lamb through the middle of the street of the city" (Revelation 22:1–2).

The tree and life-giving river dominate the new Jerusalem, making it very like the Garden of Eden—it is a garden city. There is an arc, a grand story line that runs from the garden to the garden city, set intentionally in place, framing Scripture.[2] Seeing this great arc can help us see other aspects of God at work as well.

First, one might ask: "If Eden is a paradise, then why not just stop there: great job done?" What is missing in the Garden of Eden? The answer is: us! The long arc that stretches from garden to garden city opens time and space for you, and me, and all those around us, time and space for us to share in God's great good gift of life, and to join the great procession toward living fully in God's presence.

Second, God is on a mission, and this is it: creating creatures to share the fullness of life with God and with one another. God's mission is the creation of creatures fitted for communion with God and with one another. The first communion is in Eden, full communion is in the new Jerusalem.

## The Life of Faith: Living from the Beginning, Toward the End
For Christians, all reality stretches between a beginning and a specific end, the two of them deeply, intentionally connected. This element of our faith has implications as we seek to live faithfully. The great arc of creation, filled by God's mission of creating

2. So it makes perfect sense that the resurrection of Jesus Christ—the overcoming of death—happens at a tomb that is in a garden. See John 19:41–42.

creatures fitted for communion gives context for our lives, sets us in personal relationship with God, offers us the gift of communion, and gives us the privilege of taking part knowingly in God's great mission.

*The great arc of creation gives context for our lives.* The Christian faith places us and all creatures in the widest context. The cosmos is, for Christians, not simply a random, impersonal sequence of happenings, just one thing after another. Creation is a coherent whole, like a well-told story: it has a beginning and a conclusion. Everything in between has coherence because it has a place in the story line that runs from that definite beginning to that definite conclusion. Our lives have meaning in this story, meaning rooted in the great story that God is creating. This cosmic context enables us to navigate the present. It helps us recognize where and when we are now. It helps us sort out what in our present moment is of lasting importance, and what is not.

*The great arc of creation sets us in personal relationship with God.* The great arc from garden to garden city is intensely personal. In life, at the deepest level, we have to do with a personal being, not just with impersonal material processes. This much is said repeatedly in the earlier verses of Genesis: and God *said*, and God *saw*, and God *enjoyed* its goodness. In these verses God's delight in creation is clear. Equally clear in Scripture is creation's corresponding delight in God (Psalm 19:1–6, Psalm 148, Job 38:7). Across the Bible, God is present and engaged. This means that our reading and study of Scripture help us learn to recognize God's presence also in our lives.

*The great arc of creation offers us the gift of communion.* Our place and time are among God's gifts to us, placing us in the story of God's good purposes, the story of all created things. Here and now, we begin to experience the gift of communion with God and with other people. We do not see this gift with equal clarity at all times. Sometimes it is very hard to recognize this gift. There are moments when we can no longer see, or feel, the connections that link our lives to the great story of God's mission. In such times, we look to others to see and feel it on our behalf, awaiting the day when our seeing and feeling will be restored.

*The great arc of creation gives us the privilege of taking part knowingly in God's great mission.* Faith gives us the privilege of enjoying communion with God, and with others. By faith we take part knowingly, personally with God in God's mission. God's mission is the creation of communion, and God seeks communion with us. We gather weekly for worship, we pray and read Scripture daily, to turn our attention to God, entering the communion God seeks with us.[3]

## The Church: Story Telling, Story Living

The church is the bearer of a story, the best and most basic story. This is the story of the world, the story that runs from creation to consummation. The church is the community of followers of the central figure in the story, the triune God who came among us, as one of us, in Jesus Christ. This story helps us know when, and where, and who we are. We are in the time of God's mission, when God is creating creatures fitted for communion with God and one another, and we get to be agents of that mission. The church is called and equipped to tell this story, and to live even now the communion for which God made us.

God calls and empowers the church to tell this story in three specific ways: in proclamation, telling the story to all; in our life together; and in building communities in which communion happens now.

The church is given the good work of telling the great story of God's mission in words, proclaiming the great story of which we are a part, the story of our value to the God who loves all creatures. It happens in our worship, as we turn our attention to the one who is always present to us, but from whom we are often distracted. In worship, we deepen our knowledge of God and God's mission, and we practice speaking what we know as we sing together, as we pray together, as we respond to the Word proclaimed in Scripture and sermon, as we enact the story in sacraments. Having learned,

3. These themes are found across Scripture. See, for example, Exodus 6:7; Psalm 46:10; 139; Ezekiel 34:30; Luke 24:13–35; John 14–17; Ephesians 1:16–20; Revelation 21:3.

having practiced, we are sent into the world, equipped and refreshed to tell the story in our own words and actions.

We tell the story in our life together as we seek to be communities in which all come to communion with God, and thus with all those others whom God loves. Life together in congregations and denominations is often a matter of the mundane—how will we be organized, what procedures shall we follow, who will do which chores. Yet such matters make it possible for our life together to be a foretaste of the communion to which God invites us. The way we deal with one another in such matters will be a witness, and God asks us to make it a witness to the goodness of God, rather than our own failings and frustrations.

We tell the story in our engagement with the world around us, working to help communities locally and globally be places where God's communion can flourish. So, the church sends workers where help is needed—next door or far away. The church works to encourage public systems that strengthen those across cities, states, and nations who seek communities that embody God's good purpose. The church advocates for good policies and seeks to build relationships that strengthen life together in all places.

In proclamation, life together, and engaging our world, the church serves God's mission of building communities that foreshadow the full communion we will live in the new Jerusalem.

## For Reflection and Action
1. What other places in Scripture have trees or gardens that remind you of the Garden of Eden and the garden city?


2. Consider the description of the Garden of Eden in the verses from Genesis 2, and the description of the new Jerusalem from Revelation 21 and 22. What common features are found in these two places?

3. How do you tell the story of the long arc of God's mission, from the Garden of Eden to the garden city, the new Jerusalem? Where have you encountered good tellings of that story?

4. In what ways is your congregation telling the story of God's mission?

5. How do you tell the story? Practice telling, in a simple, summary way, the great story of God's work of creation, from beginning to conclusion.

## Chapter 2

# Creatures of God: Finite and Flourishing

## Scripture

**Genesis 1:1–2:9**  God's work of creation begins by setting basic conditions, making possible a florid diversity of creatures, for whom God gives habitable habitations.

**Revelation 21:12–26**  At the culmination of creation God makes a habitable habitation, into which God gathers the glories produced by the astonishing diversity of creatures.

Related texts: Job 42:1–6; Psalm 8; Matthew 6:25–34; John 14:2–4

## Prayer

Gracious God, we claim your promise to move among us in the power of the Holy Spirit as we read and study your word. Open our ears, that we may hear you speaking to us. Open our hearts, that we might take your word to heart. Remind us that life is your gift. Strengthen our response of gratitude. Grant us wisdom that we might join your work of making spaces where communion flourishes. In the name of our Savior Jesus Christ, we pray. Amen.

## Introduction

Next comes a second theme of the Bible: God creates the basic conditions creatures need to live in communion. The Bible begins with God's creation of the world (Genesis 1:1–2:4a). These verses are rich with theological substance. This chapter will focus on one theological theme: the order in which the days of creation unfold, and what that ordering means for our understanding of ourselves (defined by what it is to be a creature) and of God (who gives us the gift of being creatures).

The story of the seven days of creation reminds us that we creatures are limited and finite. The story affirms that this is a gift—even though we often experience it as a burden. If we are to exist at all, there are certain basic conditions that we need in order to be, much less to flourish. Being finite and limited, we are fragile, vulnerable.

It is part of God's grace that God gives habitable habitations for us, spaces in which we can flourish. In these habitations, we creatures do indeed flourish, in amazing variety and diversity. The earth itself is a finite home (as has become very clear over the course of the last century). For the first couple, Adam and Eve, even the earth was a disorientingly vast space. So, God gave a smaller, sheltered place for them, the Garden of Eden. At the end, God again gives a bounded place, the new Jerusalem, now a habitation for all creatures. One element of God's mission is making habitable habitations in which creatures can respond to God's quest to create creatures fitted for communion with God and one another. Between beginning and end, in varied ways, God continues to work for the creation of habitations in which creatures will flourish.

Our second theme entails how God makes a way for creatures by setting basic boundary conditions that enable a stunning diversity of creatures to emerge, and God's provision of life-giving spaces for them.

## A Basic Theme: Creatures, Finite and Flourishing

Genesis offers two explorations of the beginnings of God's work of creation, the story of the beginning told in two ways. Chapter 1 looked at the second. Now we turn to the first, starting in the first verse of Genesis 1 and running to the first half of Genesis 2:4.

This first telling of the story of creation is carefully structured, built on repeated elements, into which advancing developments are set. The story of each day is told in a carefully structured, repeated pattern, with God as the main actor.

The *sequence* of the days is also carefully articulated, and is theologically important. The sequence tells us something about what it means for us to be creatures who are finite, limited, and vulnerable.

It starts at the beginning of the first day. The second verse of Genesis 1 describes an earth that "was a formless void," in darkness, swept by wind. "Formless void" translates the Hebrew words *tohu wabohu*. These words describe the opposite of creation: desolation, chaos, places where life cannot survive. In the Old Testament, there is an acute awareness that chaos is a constant danger, and descent into chaos a possibility, making life impossible.[1] A favorite image of this was a violent storm at sea: water threatening from above and below, confusion about what is up and what is down, complete instability, the impossibility of sighting where one is and what dangers might be near.[2] If creatures, being finite and interdependent, are to exist at all, they need a basic order. We need boundary conditions to be set and to hold. This need is also a matter of science: life as we know it on earth depends on nature functioning with certain boundary conditions: an earth whose climate is neither too hot nor too cold, a makeup of chemical elements in the proper amounts, an earth set at a distance from the sun to allow light and heat and radiation within certain boundaries.[3]

Over the first four days of creation, God sets up basic conditions for life. First, light and darkness are separated. Then waters are separated into those that lie below and those that fall from above. Dry land and water are gathered together and distinguished from one another, and the land is fertile. Light is gathered into specific sources that mark basic units of time: day and night, seasons, years.

These are the first gifts of creation. Boundary conditions are set that enable creatures to exist and flourish. The conditions are like the frame of a house. In providing them, God is making a habitable

1. Scripture tells of such a descent in Judges 19–21.
2. A storm at sea is an image across the Bible for life-threatening chaos. For storms at sea as an image of life-threatening danger see for example, Psalm 29; 46:2; 69:1–3; 77:16–20; Jonah 1. The stories of Jesus' disciples in boats caught in storms convey the sense of the storm as an experience of chaos (Mark 4:35–41; Matthew 14:28–33). The same terror can be felt in Acts 27:13–44, the storm at sea on Paul's journey to Rome.
3. This is sometimes called "fine tuning." The earth is fine-tuned, within narrow tolerances, for life as we know it to emerge in abundance. Concern about global warming is rooted in awareness that these boundary conditions are vital to life.

place for creatures, habitations suited to creaturely limitations, in which creatures can flourish. When properly set, boundary conditions enable life to flourish.

How creatures flourish within the boundary conditions set by God! Once these basic conditions are in place, a florid diversity of creatures cascades out, "cattle and creeping things and wild animals of the earth of every kind." This rich diversification is a matter to which we will return.

## The Life of Faith: The Gift of Finitude

Boundary conditions are part of what it is to be creatures. They are both a gift and a challenge. Living faithfully as creatures, dependent on boundary conditions set in such a way that life flourishes within them, calls for us to cultivate gratitude and wisdom, and join God in the work of making habitable habitations in which to live God's gift of communion.

The basic structure God puts in place in Genesis 1 is a gift. It makes life possible. The *tohu wabohu* offered no space in which creatures can flourish. God continues to give habitable habitations for creatures across the great arc from beginning to end—both real and envisioned, beginning with the Garden of Eden. The wide earth is too large for two, so God makes a shelter (Genesis 2:8). When the people of Israel are released from slavery in Egypt, they wander in the desert. In that uninhabitable space, God provides a traveling habitation for them—an encampment with a tabernacle in which God communes with them. Food and water are given as long as they are needed (Exodus 15–17; 25–28). The land where the people settle is a habitation. Zion is envisioned as a shelter in which humans will live in communion with God (for example, Isaiah 2:2–4; 35:1–10). When taken into exile in Babylon the people experience dislocation that feels like chaos, and the prophet Jeremiah tells them that God has made a place for them there, and is waiting for them to move in (Jeremiah 29:1–9). In the ministry of Jesus Christ, his followers are given one another as a place in which to dwell with God (John 15:12–17).

Scripture reveals God setting boundary conditions in other ways. The Ten Commandments mark borders (Exodus 20:1–17; Deuteronomy 5:1–21). The commandments mark out a space within which life can flourish. This understanding of the Ten Commandments runs deep in the Christian faith, particularly in the Reformed tradition. The explanation of the Ten Commandments in the Westminster Catechisms strives toward a vision of a society marked by communion and care.

Knowing ourselves to be creatures, who receive the gift of conditions that enable us not only to live, but to flourish, calls for us to respond. First, we respond with gratitude. Boundary conditions, placed to enable fullness of life, are part of God's grace. We have the privilege of responding, gratefully receiving this gift. We do so by thanking God, and acknowledging both gift and giver in our praise. We thank God by acknowledging God's commands that name ways of living that obstruct God's mission. We thank God by joining the Holy Spirit in building habitations in which all persons can live in the life-giving communion on which all creatures depend.

Second, we respond by cultivating wisdom. Wisdom grows by learning ever more deeply how to live well within the boundary conditions that make life possible. Wisdom helps us respond effectively to places in the world around us in which communion is being damaged.

## The Church: Bearing Tidings of Comfort and Joy

The word "creature" is deeply connected to the word "Creator"— etymologically and theologically. We live alongside many people who do not see or know the Creator as the divinely good and gracious one who gives the gift of life to those who are finite, limited, and vulnerable. To miss the connection between "creature" and "Creator" is to be left being a creature without the encompassing framework provided by the God who is love, who created and redeemed us. When loss and death and suffering strike, what framework is there to sustain our affirmation that our life remains preciously valuable?

Amid a world in which so many contend with finitude, limitation, and vulnerability without claiming the connection with the Creator, the church bears good news of comfort and joy.

No story in the Bible wrestles with finitude, limitation, and vulnerability as intensely as the book of Job. Job tells a story of one who suffers the destruction of his wealth and most of his possessions, the death of many of his employees, the loss of his children in a building collapse, and finally the loss of his health. This all happens, the story tells, with God's permission—a possibility many Christians have contemplated in times of hurt and loss, asking how God could have allowed this to happen to them. A few friends join Job, and over the next thirty-five chapters they argue about death, suffering, God, and creatures. Job begins the argument by cursing his birth—rejecting any notion that his life as a creature is a gift.

At the end of the book, God addresses Job directly. God does not offer any simple answers to the pressing question, "Why?" Instead, God focuses on the wider frame of creation (which we considered in chapter 1). God points to creatures that are mysterious and marvelous (humans are not the only ones who are both).

In the final chapter of the book, Job has a brief speech acknowledging the wonder of creation and the gift of life. His final line is generally translated as "therefore I despise myself, and repent in dust and ashes." Old Testament scholars have suggested, however, that a different translation is equally true to the Hebrew source. Job says, "I am comforted concerning dust and ashes." Professor Carol Newsom paraphrases this alternate translation: "I am comforted concerning my finite humanity."[4]

The church carries and proclaims the same story that God speaks to Job: the story of the wider frame of creation, and God's mission across that creation. In a world in which many of those around us live amid finitude, limitation, and vulnerability without this framework in which to weather life's harms, the church tells the story of the God who gives life as a sheer gift, who follows that gift with the building of habitations in which to make an otherwise inhospitable world fully, richly habitable. In our proclamation, in the way we live with one another, in the way we work to sustain places in which to have communion with God and one another, in all these ways the church shares the gift God has given to us.

---

4. William Morrow proposes the alternate translation. Morrow is quoted in an excellent exploration of these matters by Carol A. Newsom, "The Moral Sense of Nature: Ethics in the Light of God's Speech to Job," *The Princeton Seminary Bulletin* XV,1 (New Series 1994), 9–17. Available at http://journals.ptsem.edu/id/PSB1994151/dmd005.

## For Reflection and Action

1. Prayers of thanksgiving are an opportunity to claim the good things that are part of the gift of life God shares with creatures. A regular discipline of thanking God in prayer on a daily or weekly basis can help us recognize God's gift for what it is.

2. Footnote 2 lists some biblical passages about storms at sea. What can we learn from these stories about living faithfully in the midst of challenging times?

3. In what ways does the great story of God's creation, from beginning to end, help you to live in the face of the challenges and difficulties that mark life as a creature of God?

4. What are concrete ways in which we can join God's work of making habitable habitations for communion with God and others?

*The life of faith calls us to receive our dependence on one another and all other creatures as part of God's gift to us.*

## Chapter 3

# Creatures of God: Mutually Dependent

## Scripture

**Genesis 2:4b–9**   Creatures are dependent on one another across creation.

**1 Corinthians 12:4–31**   The church is a place that embodies the mutual dependence that gives fullness of life.

Related texts: Exodus 18:13–27; Luke 22:24–30; Romans 12:4–13

## Prayer

God our creator and redeemer, we give you thanks for the great good gift of life. We thank you that you give us the gift of one another. We thank you for Jesus Christ, in and through whom you give us the Holy Spirit, who empowers us to build relationships that enable us to be dependable, and to depend on one another for fullness of life. Make us a community that flourishes together in loving and being loved by you. In Christ's name, we pray. Amen.

## Introduction

Creatures are not capable of being self-sufficient. We cannot by ourselves provide all that we need. We are dependent on others, a world of others, if we are to live life well and fully. In the same way, all those others are dependent on us. You depend on me, I depend on you, and we depend on the others around us, both near and far. This chapter's theme is interdependence, part of God's good creation that is a focus and a concern across the Bible.

This means that you are among God's good gifts to me and to everyone else. And I am among the many, so many who are God's good gift to you. Our very identity is shaped by those around us. Our families, our communities, the regions and specific locales in which we live—all shape us, usually without our having chosen them. Interdependence is something we experience every day. When we drive down the road, we depend on others to be in the proper place on the road, and they depend on us for the same. We depend on those who make our buildings to make them soundly. We depend on those who grow and transport our food. Most of the time we simply take this thick web of interdependence for granted. Whether we notice it or not, it is one of God's gifts to us. We could not flourish without it. Nor could others flourish without the part that we contribute. When our interdependence works in the life-giving ways God intends, we can do and be more. We can flourish.

But of course, it doesn't always work in the life-giving ways God intends. Our dependence on one another makes us vulnerable. Those we depend on sometimes fail us, sometimes use our dependence on them in ways that victimize. Power to serve can be twisted into power to make others serve.

Interdependence gives each of us a part to play in the well-being of all. When someone, or many someones, do not or are not allowed to play that role, all are weakened.

## A Basic Theme: Depending on One Another

There is something odd about the description of the earth at the beginning of the second story of the creation's start (Genesis 2:4b–9). The story begins by setting the scene, telling us what time it is. We are in the "day" when the earth and the heavens are made. We are dropped into the story. The first thing the story notes about the earth is that there is no vegetation growing yet:

> when no plant of the field was yet in the earth and no herb of the field had yet sprung up. (2:5)

This lack of growth needs an explanation:

> —for the LORD God had not caused it to rain upon the earth.

This suggests that the reason no vegetation was growing was a lack of water. But (skipping over the next phrase) we are told that lack of water was not a problem:

> but a stream would rise from the earth, and water the whole face of the ground. (2:6)

There is ample water everywhere, rising from sources under the surface. The phrase in between identifies what was lacking:

> and there was no one to till the ground. (2:5b)

The Hebrew word translated *till* is used hundreds of times in the Old Testament and has a range of meanings. It often means "service," and when it is a noun it means "servant" or "slave." No vegetation has sprung forth in this highly fertile context because the vegetation depends on the one who will care for it in all the ways that farmers care for food that springs from the dirt (as they care for animals as well). The interdependence of creatures is part of the fabric of creation from its very beginnings, and that interdependence is not reserved only for humans, but stretches beyond humans, who are marked by our dependence on what is beyond the human community, just as we depend on other people.

The depth of our dependence on others is repeatedly affirmed across the Bible. When Moses is leading the people in the wilderness he begins by settling all their disputes himself; his father-in-law Jethro insists that the work must be shared with many others—a recommendation Moses puts into practice (Exodus 18:13–27). The warrior Barak is dependent on two women: the prophet-leader Deborah, and Jael (Judges 4:1–22). Isaiah 5:8 denounces those who push out others "until there is room for no one but you, and you are left to live alone in the midst of the land." Jesus instructs his disciples to be servants of one another, as he is (Mark 10:41–44, 9:33–37). Interdependence is central to the nature of the church in the New Testament letters—especially in 1 Corinthians 12 (see also Romans 12:4–8).

To be human is to be dependent on a web of others across creation, and it means many, known and unknown to us, are depending on us. For we only flourish in God's way when we are dependable, and when we depend, faithfully.

## The Life of Faith: The Gift of One Another

The story of the Garden of Eden gives a picture of interdependence working in ways that serve the flourishing of all. The human being, Adam, is put in the garden to serve it by tilling it, and trees and other vegetation flourish. The first couple, Adam and Eve, share in this service. They live dependent on one another, on the rest of creation around them, and on God.

Until they don't. The two humans together eat the fruit of "the tree of the knowledge of good and evil" (Genesis 2:17), rejecting God's command to eat of any tree in the garden *except* that one. The temptation that the serpent offers to Eve and Adam is to reject their interdependence. Beginning with their dependence on God, if they eat the forbidden fruit, "you will be like God, knowing good and evil" (Genesis 3:5). Before eating the fruit of the tree, Adam and Eve clearly experienced good. Eating the fruit does not appear to have given them any additional knowledge of good. But it does give them knowledge of evil that they did not have before. Now interdependence becomes a burden and a danger.

Dependence on one another makes us vulnerable. Sometimes we fail those who depend on us inadvertently. We do not show up on time (or at all), we forget about our obligations, we drive distracted, we lose the key email, or we make our contribution to a group effort half-heartedly. There is more than that. Sometimes those we depend on use that dependence to harm us. We see vulnerability used in these ways all around our world. Refugees driven by danger to flee, traveling out of their home, town, city, and country face other dangers as they flee and resettle. The poor lack the resources that enable those better off to hide or reduce their dependence on others, and suffer as a result. Sometimes our dependence on others becomes a burden. The elderly come to depend on others with a directness that in many cases they never experienced when they were younger. For the vulnerable, dependence on others is immediate, often starkly so.

The Old Testament books of the prophets speak persistently, uncompromisingly of God's command to care for those who are vulnerable. Thus, Jeremiah is sent to the royal throne room to tell the king and all the powerful around him:

> "Act with justice and righteousness, and deliver from the hand of the oppressor anyone who has been robbed. And do no wrong or violence to the alien, the orphan, and the widow." (Jeremiah 22:3; see also Malachi 3:5)

Jesus pointed to the offering of the widow in the Temple as a model of faithfulness (Mark 12:41–44), and the earliest church from its very beginnings cared for widows and the vulnerable (Acts 6:1–6).

The life of faith calls us to receive our dependence on one another and all other creatures as part of God's gift to us, part of what it is to be a creature of God. Growth in faithfulness to God will bring with it a growing ability to discern abuses of our mutual dependence, beginning with our own hearts and minds.

## The Church: Shared Flourishing

The church knows the goodness of creation, and it knows that interdependence is, in God's hands, part of the gift of being creatures in relationship with this God, and thus with one another, and more widely with other creatures as well. The church also knows that there is more than goodness in the world. The web of relationships made by our dependence on one another has been torn. Interdependence has been and is being refused. Interdependence has become vulnerability; our vulnerability is taken advantage of by others.

As agents of the mission of God, the church seeks in its own life and in the world around it to embody relationships that allow our dependence on one another to lead to flourishing for all. The church does this both internally and externally.

The church is called and empowered by God to be a community of communities in which the relationships of mutual dependence and flourishing found back in the Garden of Eden, and ahead in the new Jerusalem, begin to be realities here and now, in all the places where congregations gather in Jesus' name. Our life together is to be a foretaste of what God is building: communion with God and with one another. This foretaste finds its clearest, richest presence in congregations, as they respond to the moving of the Holy Spirit.

This happens, in part, in ways so familiar that we may miss their importance. Regular practices of worship make congregations places where God's communion can be tasted. We do this in the weekly lifting up together of prayer concerns. These regular prayers flow into concrete acts of care for one another—visiting in the hospital, preparing meals for those in difficult situations. Gathered around the communion table we taste God's communion with us in Jesus Christ, who came among us and gave his very life in service to us, meeting our need for the forgiveness that brings reconciliation with God and others. The way a congregation is ordered can serve to make it a place where God's communion is tasted, if that order helps the congregation remain rooted first in communion with God, and then in relationships with one another that enable each to play their distinct part in ways that sisters and brothers can rely on. This is an abiding concern of Reformed theology and church life.

God's mission, which makes the church a foretaste of communion, extends beyond the church. As agents of God's mission, the church is attentive to the world around it, starting in its neighborhood and reaching to the ends of the earth. God made all people for communion with God. The church struggles against all that destroys the communion God is creating: racism, poverty, disease, lack of education, patterns of contempt and hatred, narrow partisanship.

God calls us to "bear one another's burdens," for "in this way you will fulfill the law of Christ" (Galatians 6:2). Dependence on one another brings life, and it is what Christ calls us to do and be, for one another, and for all whom God loves.

## For Reflection and Action

1. Where do we see interdependence in the two stories of creation in Genesis 1–2?

2. Describe a person or situation in your life who embodied the interdependence that enabled themselves—and others—to flourish and bring glory to God. Is there someone you have helped to flourish and bring glory to God?

3. In what ways does your congregation show or work for the interdependence that enables flourishing?

4. Make a brief time this week to consider how you are part of a web of those who depend on one another. Name two things God has empowered you to bring to others, and two things others have been empowered to bring you. Thank God for these gifts.

*Living well amid diversity calls for holy confidence and holy curiosity.*

## Chapter 4

# Creatures of God:
# God Does Not Clone

## Scripture
**Genesis 1:22, 28; 9:7** God calls for creatures, including human beings, to share the blessing of life across generations, which are marked by increasing differentiation and complexity.

**Revelation 21:24–26** Across the great arc of God's mission the nations have generated amazing differentiation and complexity, which is so valuable that God makes a place for it in the new Jerusalem.

Related texts: Genesis 4:17–22; 5:1–32; 10:1–32; 11:1–9; Acts 2:1–21

## Prayer
Creating God, we thank you for your blessing, and for the astonishing diversity that it brings forth—creatures great and small, places comfortable and extreme, cultures and languages that vary so widely. Teach us to be different with vibrancy. Give us holy confidence and holy curiosity with which to do so. Move in us, Holy Spirit, to help us understand and know one another across differences, and to be agents of such understanding in this time. In the name of Jesus Christ, we ask these things. Amen.

# Introduction

In earlier chapters, we have considered biblical themes that stretch from the first three chapters of Genesis across Scripture, even to the final chapters of Revelation. We've looked at the garden and the garden city, anchoring the great arc of creation that stretches between them, giving direction to it all as God's mission unfolds. We've reflected on what it is to be a creature, and thus to be finite, and limited, and therefore vulnerable. We've explored our dependence on one another, dependence that is good, even as it is open to abuse.

This session takes up one more theme found in the first three chapters of Genesis, and across Scripture: God's creative power generates staggering diversification. The early anchor for this arching theme is God's blessing: "be fruitful and multiply." In Genesis 1:22, the blessing is given to the birds of the air and the creatures of the sea. In 1:28, God gives this blessing to humans.[1]

"Be fruitful and multiply." It seems plain enough. But is it? What does "multiply" mean? Identical copies? Clones? Clearly not. The first story of creation in Genesis overturns that idea: once the basic conditions for life are in place, creatures burst forth in stunning variety, creatures in the water, in the air, sea monsters and cattle and creeping things and wild animals of every kind. And not one of them is merely generic. Each has its own particular character, its own personality. This is a matter of observable fact: nature around us, when it is functioning well, generates an incredible variety of creatures, adapted to sometimes very specific conditions. We grieve and work against extinctions because we recognize the value and importance of the steady impulse to diversification that is a basic feature of the created order.

Diverse, particular, unique—and yet creatures are also similar. Every fingerprint is different, yet it is common to human beings to have fingerprints. Individuality and commonality, similarity and difference, to be a creature is to be shaped by both.

This session will consider diversification, a hallmark of God's creative mission. This hallmark is very clear in some unlikely places: the genealogies in Genesis, in a detail of the new Jerusalem, and elsewhere across the Bible.

---

1. God reaffirms the blessing to humans in the covenant God makes with Noah when the flood receded and everyone left the ark (Genesis 9:1, 7).

## A Basic Theme: Be Fruitful and . . . Diversify

"To Enoch was born Irad; and Irad was the father of Mehujael, and Mehujael the father of Methusahel . . . " (Genesis 4:18). The Bible's genealogies seem senseless: endless repetition, odd names, all connected to nothing we can connect to. Reading them our minds go numb.

But for Scripture, in both Testaments, genealogies are a way of thinking about and understanding the world. They are a form of reasoning. A form that is unfamiliar to us, a form that we don't use. We don't know what sense they have, and so they seem to have no sense. But we're wrong about that.

Between Genesis 1 and 11 there are four genealogies, two of which take up entire chapters. And each one has something to tell us about the growth and ordering of creation.

The first comes as a surprise. At the very end of the first story of creation, the story of the succession of days that is so carefully constructed and ordered, we are told: "These are the *generations* of the heavens and the earth when they were created" (2:4a). The Hebrew word translated "generations" here (the word is *toledoth*) is also used in the first verse of the chapter-long genealogies that follow (chapters 5 and 10), where it is translated "descendants." Creatures are not only given the gift of life. God's blessing ("be fruitful and diversify") gives them the gift of bringing forth new life, generations succeeding one another.[2] In that succession, across time, other creatures have the opportunity to come into existence, to have their unique, particular place and time, and thus for the diversity made possible by the basic conditions laid down by God to realize more of creation's inherent possibilities.

The other three genealogies demonstrate that God's blessing is being fulfilled. Next, in Genesis 4:17–26 the succeeding generations develop basic elements of human civilization: cities, nomadic life and herding, music, and religion. Then, in Genesis 5:1–32 the genealogy focuses on persons and their relationship to one another: humanity is diversifying into families as God's blessing has its effect. In Genesis 10:1–32 we find something

2. Old Testament scholar Claus Westermann notes that the meanings attributed by Eve to the names Cain (Genesis 4:1) and Seth (4:25) explicitly affirm that the potential to bring forth new generations is a blessing that continues in full effect after the first couple is sent out of Eden. Claus Westermann, *Genesis 1–11*, trans. by John Scullion, S.J., Continental Commentary (Minneapolis: Fortress Press, 1994), 17–18.

quite different. Now what is described for us is the development of nations. Names in this genealogy are, in many cases, names of nations: "Egypt became the father of . . ." (10:13). This genealogy specifically states that these nations not only had land of their own, but also "their own languages" (10:5, 20, 31). Even before the Tower of Babel there was a diversity of languages (we'll return to that), and with different languages come different cultures.

"Be fruitful and multiply"? A better translation is "be fruitful and diversify."

## The Life of Faith: Holy Confidence, Holy Curiosity

God's creative power and blessing generates the astonishing diversity of people and creatures that we see in the world around us. Each creature is both unique and particular, yet also similar to and fit for interdependence with one another. This diversity is a gift; it is also a persistent challenge.

A detail in the story of the new Jerusalem reveals how deeply God values the gifts of diversity. We are told that "the kings of the earth will bring their glory into it" (Revelation 21:24).[3]

This is so important that the point is repeated just two verses later: "People will bring into it the glory and the honor of the nations" (v. 26). We have seen that the rise of varied nations is part of the outworking of God's blessing in creation. Now, in the new Jerusalem, we find that the glories accumulated by the many nations are so valuable to God that God draws them into the new Jerusalem, where they are to be preserved. These glories matter to God, and are not to be destroyed. They are part of the gift of diversification, the diversity of nations and cultures.

Living well in the midst of diversity is a steady challenge. Facing that challenge calls for holy confidence and holy curiosity.

Holy confidence provides a secure sense of self that enables us to encounter those who differ from us with peace. Holy confidence is rooted in a deep understanding that we know that we are creatures of a God who has given us and others the gift of life, and that being creatures makes us fundamentally both limited and

3. I rely here on Kevin Park's wonderful homily, "The Nations Will Bring Their Glory," (https://perspectivesjournal.org/blog/2004/11/16/nations-will-bring-their-glory/). This homily has been incorporated into Kevin Park, *The Nations Will Bring Their Glory*, Theological Conversations 4 (Louisville, KY: Office of Theology & Worship, 2015).

interdependent. Knowledge of God, of the nature of God's creative work, of God's sovereignty over the creation, and of God's movement toward a specific end serves to grant us peace in the presence of our differences, especially those that are difficult. It provides solid ground, an assurance that allows us to live out of those two words that God speaks so often to people across the Bible: "fear not" (for example, Joshua 1:6–9; Psalm 23; Isaiah 43:1; Lamentations 3:55–57; Zephaniah 3:16–17; Mark 5:36; Luke 2:10). Holy confidence does not simply abandon our convictions to suit those who differ from us, nor does it refuse to do the work of understanding and learning from the convictions of those from whom we differ. It is attentive.

Attentive and inquisitive. Holy confidence makes it possible for us to have a holy curiosity about all the other creatures around us. Engaging our world and those in it is part of our faith. It is one of the reasons that the Reformed tradition (and other Christian traditions as well) has been so deeply committed to education: education teaches us about the diversity of creation. Good and faithful education also gives us helpful tools for practicing curiosity. Curiosity is holy when it never loses sight of the fact that our interest in others always happens in the context of a third one: God.

## The Church: When Together Goes Wrong

The final narrative in the first part of Genesis (Genesis 1–11) is a story about God's impulse to diversification and human rejection of that impulse. It is the story of the Tower of Babel.

At the beginning of Genesis 11 the "whole earth" migrates out of the east and decides to build a city, and a tower,

> with its top in the heavens, and let us make a name for ourselves; otherwise we shall be scattered abroad upon the face of the whole earth. (11:4)

Things have gone badly wrong. God's creative power and blessing has bubbled over and out, in exuberant diversification. This group rejects diversification, concentrating all into one people with one project. This group is driven by a compulsion to make their own name. To be known and loved by God is not enough.

In the earlier chapters God comes to humans to talk with them; this group is determined to make its own way to God (as if God is trapped in the sky). The previous chapters are thick with names, names that mean something, identifying particular people; this group is nameless, striving to name itself. Uniqueness and particularity are submerged. It is simply called "the whole earth." The great blob. Are they really "the whole earth," or do they just think of themselves as such? This aggregate is concentrated on and organized in service of a single task: building their way to god. Human beings are reduced to nameless cogs in a giant undertaking intended to glorify this anonymous mass, an embodiment of a theology wrong from bottom to top.

I once heard someone ask, "What is a poison?" The answer: "A poison is too high a concentration of an otherwise potentially good thing." Think of medicines: the dosage is crucial. Too high a concentration, and bad things happen. The same thing is true in Genesis 11. Human beings are glorious creatures (see Psalm 8). But things go wrong when we reject the diversification and unique particularity God has given each one of us.

God intervenes, dispersing this excessive concentration. Most interpreters see the arrival of different languages as a punishment. But that's too simple. There are multiple languages before Babel; Genesis 10 makes that point three times over (vv. 5, 20, 31). The different nations are differentiated in part by language: each is developing its own. Maybe before Babel there were different languages, but people were able to understand across those differences: they were multi-lingual, readily able to understand multiple languages. God's response to the Babel project is to make differences of language difficult to overcome: many people become mono-lingual. Understanding across languages and cultures is still possible, but it has become difficult.

Until the Day of Pentecost. On that day, the Holy Spirit gives the church renewed ability to understand across those differences, to be once again vibrantly interdependent. That is our calling, in a world that often seems to make us cogs, in a world rife with misunderstanding across our differences.

## For Reflection and Action

1. Why is it important that we creatures are different from one another?

2. What are some specific things that make diversity difficult in your life? What step(s) can you take to begin to overcome one or two of those difficulties?

3. How does the Christian faith help us understand people across differences of language and culture? In what ways do congregations now embody the understanding across differences of language and culture that the church was given on Pentecost (Acts 2)?

4. Make time in your schedule, each day of the week to come, to spend five minutes focusing your attention on the wide diversity that marks creation—diversity in nature and among peoples. Name something each day for which you can thank God.

For Reflection and Action:

1. Why is it important that we creatures are different from one another?

2. 

3. 

4.

*Sin is always in relation to God, because sin at its root is a turning away from God and God's good purposes for creation.*

## Chapter 5

# Sin and Redemption: God Doesn't Go Back

## Scripture
**Genesis 3:22–24**   The first humans rupture communion and are sent forward.

**John 20:24–29**   The resurrected body of Jesus reveals the meaning of redemption.

Related text: Isaiah 1:18–20

## Prayer
God of forgiveness and redemption, we thank you that you are not overcome by our sins and brokenness. Thank you for your redeeming love that drains away the deadliness of the wounds sin inflicts on us and through us. Make us a community in which sins can be acknowledged in sure confidence that you forgive them. By your Spirit empower us to be a people who find the fruit of the tree of life in all the places you are causing it to grow. In Jesus' name, we pray. Amen.

## Introduction
The great arc of God's mission from the Garden of Eden to the garden city has appeared smooth, but that's not the whole story. There is a rupture, early in the story line, and the effects of that rupture are profound and lasting. Scripture is clear: sin enters

the picture, tearing the fabric of creation. So, what does God do when the smooth arc has been ruptured? God redeems. And what does "redeemed" look like? These things will be explored in this chapter.

God's provision for creatures is abundant. The first couple is given a garden full of what they need to flourish. "You may freely eat of every tree of the garden," God tells them, except for one tree—the tree of the knowledge of good and evil:

> for in the day that you eat of it you shall die. (2:17)

They don't need the fruit of this tree for survival. Eating the fruit is a rejection of their status as creatures. It is a desire to be something else—to be "like God"—except that they are already in the image of God (1:27). So perhaps the desire is to be *even more* like God. It turns out eating the fruit is not a good way to become more like God.

Their action has its effects that do and do not fit what God or the serpent promised. They already knew good. Knowing evil may give them something else in common with God, but not anything that gives them abundant life. God has warned: "in the day that you eat of it you shall die" (Genesis 2:17). It's not at once clear what that "death" would be, though the story eventually tells the couple. It does not mean that they drop dead the moment they take the bite. It means that interdependence has become difficult. The soil that waited for the human being to spring forth vegetation will no longer reliably spring forth. The relationship of the man and the woman gains difficulties. And, they will no longer inhabit the garden, that supremely habitable habitation.

## A Basic Theme: Sin and Salvation

The word that the Christian faith uses to talk about the first couple ignoring God's instruction and eating fruit from the one tree they were not to is "sin."

The meaning of "sin" in the Christian faith is not obvious, and is easily missed. The common usage of "sin" today virtually reverses the meaning it has for Christian faith. Often, we find it used to describe desserts: "sinfully rich." It suggests something intensely desirable, something that goes against (some set of) rules, something that (for some reason) we should not eat. Something that, with a little nudge from advertising and our own desires, we will eat anyway.

For the Christian faith, sin is not just about rule-keeping. Sin is always in relation to God, because sin at its root is a turning away from God and God's good purposes for creation. It rejects creaturely finitude as worthless. We see this in the story of Babel, explored in chapter 4. On the one hand, the mass gathered there rejects creatureliness by striving to be something more. At the same time, those gathered at Babel reject creatureliness by becoming something less, subsuming their distinct individual identity into an anonymous mass. (Indeed, the two forms of rejection often go together.)

The effects of sin (those we commit, those committed against us) are felt in our creaturely finitude. Our finitude and limitation come to burden and bind us. Our interdependence is no longer the means of mutual flourishing, but the opening for abuse suffered and perpetrated.

Above all, sin throws us off course. When we come to Genesis 3, it looks like God's mission has crashed. If the mission of God runs from the Garden of Eden to the garden city, the new Jerusalem, what does God do?

The amazing thing about what happens next is that God shows no interest in getting human beings back to Eden—as if the only path from garden to garden city starts in Eden. Salvation doesn't mean getting back to where and who we were before. God does not send us back. God moves humanity forward from where we landed after we ruptured communion. The God who created all things is perfectly capable of fulfilling God's mission by charting a course from the place where we land after we've thrown ourselves off course.

A curious part of Genesis 3 comes at the end: at the entrance of the garden God "placed the cherubim, and a sword flaming and turning to guard the way to the tree of life" (3:24). Often that sword is seen as protection for the tree of life. But perhaps not. Perhaps it is there in case human beings decide the only place they can find the tree of life is by going back. No—the tree of life is planted elsewhere, somewhere on the way forward. So, there will be manna and quail in the wilderness (Exodus 16). So, Jesus will say, "I am the bread of life" (John 6:35). So Revelation tells us "On either side of the river is the tree of life" (22:2).

## The Life of Faith: The Marks of Salvation

Salvation doesn't mean returning to the situation before sin happened. Redemption doesn't require erasing the past. Redemption overcomes the effects of sin, even when those effects leave their mark on us. God finds us where sin dumps us out, and moves us toward the end from there. This is important, because our past is part of who we are, even the parts where we went (or were thrown) off course.

What do salvation and redemption look like? The Greek word translated "save" is also sometimes translated "heal." The New Testament gives glimpses of salvation and redemption in the healing of two persons.

First, consider a woman who had been suffering from internal bleeding—hemorrhages—for over a decade (Mark 5:25–34). She had spent all her money seeking a cure, without success. Her condition rendered her ritually unclean, making social contact fraught with difficulty. While Jesus, surrounded by a large crowd, is on his way to heal someone else, she bravely comes up behind him, touches his clothes, and is healed. Her bleeding stops. Jesus knows that someone has touched him for healing. He asks who it was, causing consternation. In the end, the woman comes forward, and is blessed by Jesus, now fully healed. While there is no going back to her past situation, there is a present in which she has been made ready for the renewal of communion. Sometimes redemption restores.

Second, consider the resurrected body of Jesus.[1] Even after resurrection, his body is marked by the wounds received during his crucifixion. Those wounds were deadly—places where life flowed out of him. Now they are deadly no more. They have lost their power to kill, and instead they now have been incorporated into his identity.

Sometimes redemption renders that which was deadly, inert. Sometimes it drains wounds of their power to kill, even when the

---

1. I am indebted on this point to Beth Felker Jones, *Marks of His Wounds: Gender Politics and Bodily Resurrection* (Oxford: Oxford University Press, 2007).

marks of the wounds remain. "Where, O death, is your victory? Where, O death, is your sting?"

This is what salvation and redemption look like. There are some cases, like the woman whose hemorrhages are healed, in which the damage is completely repaired. There are some cases, like the resurrected Jesus, when the marks of wounds remain, with their death-dealing power extinguished.

The Christian life is the life of the redeemed, those who embrace the way of life found in following the resurrected One, Jesus Christ, who bears the marks of wounds that have been overcome in fullness of life. As such we are called, indeed empowered, to be forthright about sin and its effects, starting in our own lives. We can face unafraid the damage our sin and the sins of others have done. Confession of our sins becomes part of draining death from that which would destroy. We do so as people who are also called to be forthright about God's salvation and redemption in and through Jesus Christ. We know God's love and forgiveness are unshaken by sin and its effects.

## The Church: The Community of the Redeemed

God's ability to deal with our sin is never in doubt. The pressing question is not: "Will God be able to deal with my sin and its effects?" The answer to that question is sure and certain: Yes. The true question is, "Can I (or we) handle acknowledging our sin, its effects, and God's saving response?" The answer to that question is all too often in doubt. That's because the confession of sin shakes us.

In Reformed orders of congregational worship, there is an element designed to help us at precisely this point: the order for confession of sin. It starts with a call to confession, which takes the form of a brief proclamation of the gospel, assuring the congregation of God's forgiveness and love. For example:

> If we say that we have no sin, we deceive ourselves, and the truth is not in us. If we confess our sins, [God] who is faithful and just will forgive us our sins and cleanse us from all unrighteousness. (1 John 1:8–9)

Only on the solid ground of the gospel can we acknowledge (especially publicly) that we have sinned, that we are sinners.

The confession of sin follows. In congregations that regularly include a shared confession of sin, it is possible to lose track of the import of this act. To confess our sin is to confess our failures, our brokenness, and the brokenness of the world around us.

An assurance of pardon then follows. This order for confession of sin began with assurance of forgiveness; we nevertheless need, having acknowledged our sin, to hear again God's forgiving love.

Then, having confessed and been assured of forgiveness, the commandment of God (the Ten Commandments, or Jesus' Great Commandments) is spoken to us, calling us to live forward in a new way, walking toward the new Jerusalem.

The church bears the knowledge that sin is a reality, that sin always has to do with God, and that sin is not just in other people and their actions, but also in ourselves (me, and you). At the same time, the church is the community that knows Jesus Christ, and in knowing Jesus Christ knows that God's forgiveness is more powerful than any sin. Gathered in Jesus Christ, the church is the place where sin, our sins (my individual sins and the sins we share in together), are no longer something we dare not admit, to others or ourselves. Here sins can be named, and in forgiveness their destructive power drained away. Here the effects of sin can be faced and overcome. Here we are freed and empowered to live together the communion with God and all others that is God's desire for and good gift to us.

The church proclaims this knowledge—of sin and the forgiveness that overwhelms sin—in our words, in our life together, and in our engagement with the world. When the knowledge of sin is working well, it gives us a humility that strengthens the holy confidence and curiosity explored in chapter 4. Knowledge of our sin keeps holy confidence from becoming unholy conceit; it sustains holy curiosity when we find that sin is indeed present in others, reminding us that just as God does not recoil when finding sin in us, neither should we recoil when we meet sin in others.

## For Reflection and Action

1. What are the effects of sin for Adam and Eve, and in the building of the Tower of Babel?

2. Why is it important that the resurrected Jesus still bears the marks of the wounds he received in his crucifixion?

3. How does the church's proclamation of the gospel in words and in its life together make the confession of sin possible? How is that happening in your congregation?

4. Confessing our sins has been a basic spiritual practice for the church since its beginnings. It addresses those things that have ruptured our communion with God and others. This week add a brief confession to your daily prayer, or reflect on how your existing practice of confession sustains communion with God and others.

*In Jesus Christ, the personal presence of God has a*
*particular face, and a specific name. This one is*
*Immanuel, God with us.*

## Chapter 6

# Sending, Gathering, Sending Again: The Heartbeat of the Mission of God

## Scripture
**John 1:1–16** Jesus promises us his presence at the beginning, and along the way.

**John 14:1–7, 25–31** Jesus helps us on the way, even to the end.

Related texts: Isaiah 65:17–25; 1 Peter 2:9; Revelation 1:8, 22:12

## Prayer
Jesus, you who are before, alongside, and ahead of us, we thank you for your presence with us. We claim the promise of your Holy Spirit, whom you send to teach us and to strengthen us to be vibrant agents of your mission. In our reading of Scripture and our conversation about life in you, help us to come to see your face and hear your voice ever more clearly, that we might follow you more nearly, and enjoy more fully the vibrant life for which you created us. Amen.

## Introduction
This study has focused on themes that start in Genesis 1–11 and span the Bible.

The narrative arc that spans the Bible is anchored in the Garden of Eden at the beginning, and in the garden city, the new Jerusalem, at the end. The tree of life grows between the two. From beginning to end, all creation unfolds, opening time and space for creatures to receive the gift of life, to be fitted to join in communion with God and one another, called to learn from God the ways of communion. We learn amid finitude and interdependence. We learn this way in a world marked by sin, by rejection of our creatureliness, seeking to be something more, or trying to be something less than creatures of God.

The early chapters of Genesis tell us of God setting in motion a divine mission to create creatures fitted for communion with God and one another. In the book of Revelation, especially its final chapters, this narrative arc finds its end-point in the garden city, the new Jerusalem, where all will live in the fullness of that communion for which all were being prepared. In between beginning and end, there is time for you and me and all creatures to be given the gift of life. In that in-between, God's continuing creative power is marked by abundance and diversification, the exuberant growth of individual creatures, each unique and particularized, and at the same time marked by things we are in common.

During the unfolding, God has called forth a people of God to be agents of God's mission. The people of ancient Israel, the Jewish people, joined in and through Jesus Christ by the church. God is always present and at work across creation; it is the people of God who recognize, name, and call attention to God and God's presence. In doing so, one name is ever spoken by the church: Jesus Christ.

## A Basic Theme: Jesus Christ, the Face of God with Us

The mission of God is not mechanical, mindlessly spinning along until it breaks down, randomly bringing things together in an impersonal way. God engages the world personally, in relationship. Communion is built on personal connection. In Jesus Christ, we find that the personal presence of God has a particular face, and a specific name. This one is Immanuel, God with us.

The personal presence of Jesus Christ at the beginning, at the end, and along the way between is especially clear in the Gospel of John. It shows us that Jesus Christ is there across the great arc from garden to garden city.

*In the beginning was the Word, and the Word was with God, and the Word was God* (John 1:1). Jesus Christ is present at the beginning of the mission of God, laying down the boundary conditions in which creaturely life will not only be possible, but will flourish. To do so marks Jesus Christ as God, something explored and elaborated in the doctrine of the Trinity.

*In my Father's house there are many dwelling places. If it were not so, would I have told you that I go to prepare a place for you?* (John 14:2). As we saw in considering the two stories of beginnings in the book of Genesis, part of God's good provision for creatures is making habitable habitations for them. We saw the same thing in the final chapters of the book of Revelation, in the new Jerusalem. There again a habitable habitation is being made for creatures—though now on a vast scale. In these verses, Jesus tells a message entirely in line with those final chapters of Revelation, only in this case we see how deeply personal God's care is.

*He was in the world, and the world came into being through him; yet the world did not know him* (John 1:10). In eating the fruit of the one tree they were told not to, the first couple was rejecting their creatureliness, and in so doing they weren't just breaking a rule. They were rejecting their relationship with God. That same rejection comes clear in the life of Jesus. It is not just one particular group that rejects God in rejecting Jesus Christ. The world rejects him. The rupture of communion is personal, and remains a problem to be overcome. God's commitment to overcoming this rupture is clear in Jesus Christ, who comes among creatures as one of us, sharing our finitude and our interdependence, doing so without turning against God and the good gift of creatureliness. Thus Jesus bears, even in the resurrection, the wounds inflicted by a world shaped by the tears in the fabric of communion.

*Abide in me as I abide in you* (John 15:4a). God's commitment to communion with us is enduring and reliable. In the life, death, and resurrection of Jesus Christ, God's commitment to communion is real and accessible. Here God becomes one of the human agents of God's mission, showing us how to do that and do that well.

## The One Who Is There

The Christian life is the promise of communion with God who is our creator, who loves us in Jesus Christ. Relationship with God in Jesus Christ is personal in ways that run from easily graspable to deeper than we can imagine. The God who in and through Jesus Christ comes to us in bread and wine that we can take in our hands is the God speaking to Job out of the whirlwind. The Gospel of John is clear: In the beginning, and in the end, and all along the way between them, we have to do with One who is personal.

Funerals remind us that this is so. Funerals are moments when we stand at the boundary line between life and death. We the living gather to remember the one who has died, and to mark the passage of this person across that line, going forward ahead of us. And we look across that line. Some of the questions we ask as we look are "what" or "why" questions. What happens there? What is it like there, on the other side? Why? Why this person, why now, why in this way?

Scripture is deeply concerned with the answer to a different question, a question that is central: "Who?" Our faith assures us that there is One there on the other side, gone on ahead, now awaiting us: "I go to prepare a place for you" and "I will come again and will take you to myself, so that where I am, there you may be also" (John 14:2–3). Jesus' concern is not only with the "many mansions" being prepared there. His concern is with the communion he and his followers have with one another. As we stand at the boundary between life and death, looking across, what the Christian faith knows is that there is One there looking back at us, Jesus Christ, God with us.

Scripture provides the essential information for learning the contours of this face. In its narratives, its commandments and laws, its love poetry and wisdom sayings, even in its genealogies, Scripture is showing the features of God, features that take shape in Jesus Christ. What we thus discover is that the face we see looks much like the people and the moments in and through whom Jesus has been active in our lives, fitting us for communion in all its fullness.

The Christian life is lived in relationship with Jesus Christ, and thereby in communion with God. It is an invitation to grow in our capacity for deep relationship with God and with all God's creatures. It invites us to love the One whose face we see in the beginning, at the end, and all along the way in between.

## The Church: Sending, Gathering, Sending Again

A basic pattern in the Christian life shapes the life of congregations: sending out and gathering back in, gathered to be sent out again, sent to gather in. In its sheer regular repetition, we tend to take the meaning of this basic pattern for granted. This is right and good: in a similar way, we don't make our heart beat by willing it to do so. It happens apart from our willing—a very good thing. The congregation goes forth into the week, and it returns a week later, and worships again, living its life. Congregations are sent out into the world to be agents of the mission of God, who is creating creatures fitted for communion with God and one another. God is at work on this mission in every moment, and invites us to be brought into that mission in each of our days. The invitation is extended by Jesus Christ, whose call comes to us: "Follow me." Accepting this invitation places us among the followers of Jesus Christ, who embrace and work to embody the call to communion with God and with all others.

The sacraments embraced by Reformed theology—baptism and the Lord's Supper—follow this same pattern. Baptism is the sacrament of gathering in, an action by which God marks one as part of the body of Christ, and thus part of the community of agents of God's mission. Against the rupture of sin that undoes communion and sets us against one another, God in and through Jesus Christ gathers the church to live in true communion. The resurrected Jesus Christ sends the Holy Spirit to empower us to live in this way. The Lord's Supper is the regular shared meal that enacts communion with God and one another. Together we are fed, spiritually nurtured by Jesus Christ, given strength for living as part of the community of agents of God's mission.

When we understand ourselves as members of congregations sent into the world, marked by baptism, and nourished by the Lord's Supper, it helps us see places in the world around us where agents of God's mission are needed. We notice those around us who are cut off from communion with others. Agents of God's mission work to make communion a reality for all. We feel acutely the pain of division and divisiveness, the percolating outrage and anger of one group toward another that so deeply marks our time, the use of power to advance one group at the expense of others. Agents of God's mission refuse the rage that seeks to isolate and diminish those with whom we disagree. Having been baptized in water, we will be attentive to water in all places, asking whether it is fit for use in baptism, and if not why not, considering what may need to be done to make it so.

Sending and gathering and sending, the church serves God's mission in the world, sustained by God's basic patterns of life and well-being.

## For Reflection and Action

1. How does Jesus Christ help us understand the long arc of God's mission in creation?

2. As you go forth from weekly worship, how can you carry reminders each day that you are an agent of the mission of God, who is personally present to you in and through Jesus Christ?

3. What congregational practices help you encounter Jesus Christ, in and through whom God is personally present to us and to all creation?

4. Take a brief time to remember passages in the Bible that have been significant to you in helping you see Jesus clearly. Remember some of the people through whom God has loved you. Give thanks to God for each one.

# Group Gatherings

Eva Stimson

# The Great Arc of Creation: From Garden to Garden City

## Main Idea
A great narrative arc runs from the Garden of Eden to the garden city, the new Jerusalem. This is the arc of God's mission throughout creation: the creation of creatures fitted for communion with God and with one another.

## Preparing to Lead
- Read and reflect on chapter 1, "The Great Arc of Creation: From Garden to Garden City."
- Review this plan for the group gathering, and select questions and activities that you will use.
- What other questions, issues, or themes occur to you from your reflection?

## Gathering
- Provide name tags and pens as people arrive.
- Provide simple refreshments; ask a volunteer to bring refreshments for the next gathering.
- Agree on simple ground rules and organization (for example, time to begin and end; location for gatherings; welcoming of all points of view; confidentiality; and so on). Encourage participants to bring their study books and Bibles.
- Review the gathering format: Gathering, Opening Worship, Conversation, and Conclusion.

## Opening Worship
**Prayer** (unison)
Gracious and loving God, source of life, as we turn to your word draw us deeper into communion with you, that we might be

more fully in communion with all those who love and follow you. Empower us to be effective and faithful agents of your work to gather all into the future full communion with you and one another. This we ask in the name of our Savior, Jesus Christ. Amen.

## Prayerful, Reflective Reading
- Read Revelation 21:9–14; 22:1–5 aloud.
- Invite all to reflect for a few minutes in silence.
- After reflection time, invite all to listen for a word or phrase as the passage is read again and to reflect on that word or phrase in silence.
- Read the passage a third time, asking all to offer a silent prayer following the reading.
- Invite volunteers to share the word or phrase that spoke most deeply to them.

## Prayer
Loving God, hear our prayers today as we seek to follow you more faithfully:

(*spoken prayers may be offered*)

Hear us now as we pray together, saying, Our Father . . .

## Conversation
- Introduce chapter 1, "The Great Arc of Creation: From Garden to Garden City." Share observations, reflections, and insights.
- Review "A Basic Theme: The Garden of Eden and the Garden City" (pp. 2–3). Share these key points:
  a. The Garden of Eden is present in the new Jerusalem. Genesis 2 is echoed in Revelation 21 and 22.
  b. The course of creation, from beginning to end, has direction and shape.
  c. The arc of God's mission throughout creation is the creation of creatures fitted for communion with God and with one another.
- Form two groups, with one making a list of the features of Eden (Genesis 2:4–15), and others making a list of the features of the new Jerusalem (Revelation 21:9–14; 22:1–5).

Compare the two lists. Consider other places in the Bible where features that are present in both passages are important: water that brings life, food provided by God, standing in the presence of God.

- Review "The Life of Faith: Living from the Beginning, Toward the End" (pp. 3–5). Ask:

   *What difference does the arc of God's mission make for how we live out the faith?*

   *What help does it provide?*

- Review "The Church: Story Telling, Story Living" (pp. 5–6). Ask:

   *How can we communicate the strength and wholeness that comes from living life within the framework offered by the movement from Eden to the new Jerusalem?*

## Conclusion
As a group, practice telling, in a simple, summary way, the great story of God's work of creation, from beginning to conclusion.

## Passing the Peace
The peace of Christ be with you.
   And also with you.
**Amen.**

# Creatures of God: Finite and Flourishing

## Main Idea

The Bible begins with God's creation of the world. Genesis 1:1–2:4a are rich with theological substance. This gathering will focus on one theological theme: the order in which the days of creation unfold, and what that ordering means for us.

## Preparing to Lead

- Read and reflect on chapter 2, "Creatures of God: Finite and Flourishing."
- Review this plan for the group gathering, and select questions and activities that you will use. Bring a ball of yarn.
- What other questions, issues, or themes occur to you from your reflection?

## Gathering

- Provide name tags and pens as people arrive.
- Offer simple refreshments if other arrangements for refreshments have not been made; ask a volunteer to bring refreshments for the next gathering.
- Review the ground rules and organization (for example, time to begin and end the gathering; location for meetings; welcoming of all points of view; confidentiality; and so on). Encourage participants to bring their study books and Bibles.
- Review the gathering format: Gathering, Opening Worship, Conversation, and Conclusion.

## Opening Worship

**Prayer** (unison)

Gracious God, we claim your promise to move among us in the power of the Holy Spirit as we read and study your word. Open

52

our ears, that we may hear you speaking to us. Open our hearts, that we might take your word to heart. Remind us that life is your gift. Strengthen our response of gratitude. Grant us wisdom that we might join your work of making spaces where communion flourishes. In the name of our Savior Jesus Christ, we pray. Amen.

## Prayerful, Reflective Reading
- Read Genesis 1:1–2:4a aloud.
- Invite all to reflect for a few minutes in silence.
- After reflection time, invite all to listen for a word or phrase as the passage is read again and to reflect on that word or phrase in silence.
- Read the passage a third time, asking all to offer a silent prayer following the reading.
- Invite volunteers to share the word or phrase that spoke most deeply to them.

## Prayer
Loving God, hear our prayers today as we seek to follow you more faithfully:

(*spoken prayers may be offered*)

Hear us now as we pray together, saying, Our Father . . .

## Conversation
- Introduce chapter 2, "Creatures of God: Finite and Flourishing" (pp. 9–15). Share observations, reflections, and insights.
- Review the Introduction (pp. 9–10). Share these key points:
  a. The focus here is on the first story of creation, and especially the order of the seven days.
  b. God puts boundary conditions in place, setting limitations.
  c. From within the boundaries, a florid diversity bursts forth in ways that embody God's grace.
- Review "A Basic Theme: Creatures, Finite and Flourishing" (pp. 10–12).
- Ask the group to outline what happens on each of the days of creation in Genesis 1:1–2:4a. Then, turn to Revelation 21:12–26 and consider the role of boundary conditions and diversity in that passage.

- Review "The Life of Faith: The Gift of Finitude" (pp. 12–13). Explore ways that we are tempted to try to ignore, or overcome our finitude. Finitude is part of what it is to be a creature, and is part of God's grace, even when that grace is difficult.
- Identify what the gift of finitude means for the Christian life. Consider how boundary conditions are part of God's provision for us.
- Wonder how gratitude and wisdom are central to our response to God's grace. Ask:

  *What does gratitude for God's boundary conditions and flourishing look like?*

- Review "The Church: Bearing Tidings of Comfort and Joy" (pp. 13–14).
- Recall the story of Job to explore the difficulties we sometimes have accepting being finite and limited. Ask volunteers to read aloud the following:
  a. Job 30:16–23
  b. Job 38:4–12 (note the parallels to Genesis 1)
  c. Job 42:1–6
  d. Job 42:7–9.

  Ponder questions that probe our discomfort with finitude, and what it means that meeting God offers us comfort with our finitude.

- Many people among us and around us are in moments when finitude is a burden. Imagine ways that we could proclaim God's comfort and joy to people who are in such straits. Ask:

  *What are concrete ways in which we can join God's work of making habitable habitations for communion with God and others?*

## Conclusion

Gather in a circle, facing inward. Name something that God created and toss the ball of yarn to someone. Repeat until the web of life is complete. Close with a prayer of thanksgiving.

## Passing the Peace
The peace of Christ be with you.
    And also with you.
**Amen.**

# Creatures of God: Mutually Dependent

## Main Idea
Interdependence is a primary aspect of what it means to be a creature. Being finite, creatures cannot exist in complete independence. We are dependent on other creatures, particularly on other people.

## Preparing to Lead
- Read and reflect on chapter 3, "Creatures of God: Mutually Dependent."
- Review this plan for the group gathering, and select questions and activities that you will use.
- What other questions, issues, or themes occur to you from your reflection?

## Gathering
- Offer name tags and pens as people arrive.
- Provide simple refreshments if other arrangements for refreshments have not been made; ask a volunteer to bring refreshments for the next gathering.
- Review the ground rules and organization (for example, time to begin and end the gathering; location for meetings; welcoming of all points of view; confidentiality; and so on). Encourage participants to bring their study books and Bibles.
- Review the format for these gatherings: Gathering, Opening Worship, Conversation, and Conclusion.

## Opening Worship
### Prayer (unison)
God our creator and redeemer, we give you thanks for the great good gift of life. We thank you that you give us the gift of one

another. We thank you for Jesus Christ, in and through whom you give us the Holy Spirit, who empowers us to build relationships that enable us to be dependable, and to depend on one another for fullness of life. Make us a community that flourishes together in loving and being loved by you. In Christ's name, we pray. Amen.

## Prayerful, Reflective Reading

- Read Revelation 21:24–26 aloud.
- Invite all to reflect for a few minutes in silence.
- After reflection time, invite all to listen for a word or phrase as the passage is read again and to reflect on that word or phrase in silence.
- Read the passage a third time, asking all to offer a silent prayer following the reading.
- Invite volunteers to share the word or phrase that spoke most deeply to them.

## Prayer

Loving God, hear our prayers today as we seek to follow you more faithfully:

(*spoken prayers may be offered*)

Hear us now as we pray together, saying, Our Father . . .

## Conversation

- Introduce chapter 3, "Creatures of God: Mutually Dependent" (pp. 17–23). Share observations, reflections, and insights.
- Review the Introduction (pp. 17–18). Share these key points:
  a. Living well requires that we not only acknowledge in our thoughts, but live out in our actions and relationships our dependence on others.
  b. This is not only a matter of us depending on others. They are dependent on us.
  c. God calls us to see that others need us and what we have to offer.
- Review "A Basic Theme: Depending on One Another" (pp. 18–20). Consider the implications of the second story about creation (Genesis 2) in which vegetation doesn't spring forth, despite fertile conditions; it depends on the presence of one to tend it. There is a symbiosis. Name other examples of

interdependence in Genesis 1–3. Read 1 Corinthians 12:4–13 and identify how interdependence is important to the life of the church.

- Wonder together how the Bible affirms diversification, while also condemning divisiveness. As:

    *How are diversification and divisiveness different?*

- Review "The Life of Faith: The Gift of One Another" (pp. 20–21). Name different ways that interdependence is part of the Christian life. Questions might invite participants to talk about how they see interdependence playing out in their own lives as they seek to live faithfully, noting both what is good about it and how it can go wrong. Ask:

    *What are some specific things that make diversity difficult in your life?*

    *What step(s) can you take to begin to overcome one or two of those difficulties?*

- Review "The Church: Shared Flourishing" (pp. 21–22). Think about how the church is to be a place where interdependence serves flourishing, and protects vulnerability. Ask:

    *How does the Christian faith help us understand people across differences of language and culture?*

    *In what ways do congregations now embody the understanding across differences of language and culture that the church was given on Pentecost (Acts 2)?*

## Conclusion

Name teachers who have influenced your life, pastors who have guided you in the faith, and persons who encourage and support you. Offer a prayer of thanksgiving for them.

## Passing the Peace

The peace of Christ be with you.
    And also with you.
**Amen.**

# Creatures of God:
# God Does Not Clone

## Main Idea
Unity and diversity concern what creatures have in common and what makes each of us particular and unique. Central to this exploration are the words of blessing/command from God, "Be fruitful and diversify" (Genesis 1:28, author's translation).

## Preparing to Lead
- Read and reflect on chapter 4, "Creatures of God: God Does Not Clone."
- Review this plan for the group gathering, and select questions and activities that you will use.
- What other questions, issues, or themes occur to you from your reflection?

## Gathering
- Provide name tags and pens as people arrive.
- Provide simple refreshments if other arrangements for refreshments have not been made; ask a volunteer to bring refreshments for the next gathering.
- Review the ground rules and organization (for example, time to begin and end the gathering; location for meetings; welcoming of all points of view; confidentiality; and so on). Encourage participants to bring their study books and Bibles.
- Review the format for these gatherings: Gathering, Opening Worship, Conversation, and Conclusion.

## Opening Worship
**Prayer** (unison)
Creating God, we thank you for your blessing, and for the astonishing diversity that it brings forth—creatures great and small,

places comfortable and extreme, cultures and languages that vary so widely. Teach us to be different with vibrancy. Give us holy confidence and holy curiosity with which to do so. Move in us, Holy Spirit, to help us understand and know one another across difference, and to be agents of such understanding in this time. In the name of Jesus Christ, we ask these things. Amen.

## Prayerful, Reflective Reading

- Read Genesis 11:1–9 aloud.
- Invite all to reflect for a few minutes in silence.
- After reflection time, invite all to listen for a word or phrase as the passage is read again and to reflect on that word or phrase in silence.
- Read the passage a third time, asking all to offer a silent prayer following the reading.
- Invite volunteers to share the word or phrase that spoke most deeply to them.

## Prayer

Loving God, hear our prayers today as we seek to follow you more faithfully:

(*spoken prayers may be offered*)

Hear us now as we pray together, saying, Our Father . . .

## Conversation

- Introduce chapter 4, "Creatures of God: God Does Not Clone" (pp. 25–31). Share observations, reflections, and insights.
- Review the Introduction (p. 26). Share these key points:
  a. Unity and diversity concern what creatures have in common and what makes each of us particular and unique.
  b. Previous chapters in this book (the flourishing enabled by boundary conditions set according to God's grace and the interdependence that is part of our finitude) give a foundation for this chapter.
  c. Central to this exploration are the words of blessing/command from God, "Be fruitful and diversify," the genealogies (especially in Genesis 5 and 10), and Revelation 21:24–26.

- Review "A Basic Theme: Be Fruitful and . . . Diversify" (pp. 27–28). Read and examine the relevant Bible passages—or at least part of them. First, there are the "Be fruitful" verses: Genesis 1:22, 28, and 9:7. Basic questions can be asked:

  *What does it mean that non-human creatures are given this same command? When Genesis says, "fill the earth," what do we believe God intends? Overrunning?*

  *For the verses from Revelation, why does God preserve these treasures, which God surely doesn't need in any meaningful sense?*

- Compare the genealogies in Genesis 5 and 10 to see how they show God's blessing/command being fulfilled, reading together small parts of these chapters (for example, 5:3–11 and 10:13–20 are thick with names, many of which are challenging to pronounce, but that particularity is part of the point).
- Review "The Life of Faith: Holy Confidence, Holy Curiosity" (pp. 28–29). Explore together how a Christian lives faithfully amid diversities of language and culture. In addition to holy curiosity and confidence, participants might have other qualities they would suggest. Difficulties in dealing with diversity might also be discussed.
- Review "The Church: When Together Goes Wrong" (pp. 29–30). Wonder together how Christians gathered in congregations can pursue understanding across differences of language and culture. Congregations sometimes open their worship space to be used by gathered congregations who wish to worship in a different language: questions might probe such relationships, to consider how such situations could build holy curiosity and confidence.

## Conclusion
Sing together "For the Beauty of the Earth," "How Great Thou Art, or some other song that celebrates the wonders of creation.

## Passing the Peace
The peace of Christ be with you.
    And also with you.
**Amen.**

# Sin and Redemption: God Doesn't Go Back

## Main Idea

The primal rupture occurs when the first couple decides to disobey God's instruction to them—God's command not to eat of the tree of the knowledge of good and evil. This act is a rejection of their creatureliness: they want to be (more) "like God." God sends us forward from the place our sin spins us off to.

## Preparing to Lead

- Read and reflect on chapter 5, "Sin and Redemption: God Doesn't Go Back."
- Review this plan for the group gathering, and select questions and activities that you will use.
- What other questions, issues, or themes occur to you from your reflection?

## Gathering

- Provide name tags and pens as people arrive.
- Provide simple refreshments if other arrangements for refreshments have not been made; ask a volunteer to bring refreshments for the next gathering.
- Review the ground rules and organization (for example, time to begin and end the gathering; location for meetings; welcoming of all points of view; confidentiality; and so on). Encourage participants to bring their study books and Bibles.
- Review the format for these gatherings: Gathering, Opening Worship, Conversation, and Conclusion.

## Opening Worship

**Prayer** (unison)

God of forgiveness and redemption, we thank you that you are not overcome by our sins and brokenness. Thank you for your redeeming love that drains away the deadliness of the wounds sin inflicts on us and through us. Make us a community in which sins can be acknowledged in sure confidence that you forgive them. By your Spirit empower us to be a people who find the fruit of the tree of life in all the places you are causing it to grow. In Jesus' name, we pray. Amen.

## Prayerful, Reflective Reading

- Read Genesis 3:14–19 aloud.
- Invite all to reflect for a few minutes in silence.
- After reflection time, invite all to listen for a word or phrase as the passage is read again and to reflect on that word or phrase in silence.
- Read the passage a third time, asking all to offer a silent prayer following the reading.
- Invite volunteers to share the word or phrase that spoke most deeply to them.

## Prayer

Loving God, hear our prayers today as we seek to follow you more faithfully:

(*spoken prayers may be offered*)

Hear us now as we pray together, saying, Our Father . . .

## Conversation

- Introduce chapter 5, "Sin and Redemption: God Doesn't Go Back" (pp. 33–39). Share observations, reflections, and insights.
- Review the Introduction (pp. 33–34). Share these key points:
  a. Chapters 1–4 have focused on continuities: themes that stretch across the Bible and across history. Chapter 5 turns to ruptures that threaten to destroy continuity.
  b. Turning away from God is sin, a term that needs definition these days because it is regularly used in ways very much at odds with the Christian usage.
  c. In the aftermath of sin God does not send us back to some place before the sin occurred. God sends us forward from the place our sin spins us off to.

- Review "A Basic Theme: Sin and Salvation" (pp. 34–36). Invite participants to consider the consequences of sin found in Genesis 3:14–19. These verses show that sin distorts our interdependence and diversity. The fruitful interdependence between farmer and plants now becomes difficult, the first couple will bring forth children (new human life) but only with difficulty, humans and snakes become dangerous to one another. The first couple doesn't drop dead when they eat the fruit (which would be one interpretation of Genesis 2:17), so participants might discuss the forms death takes. Ask:

  *What does the first couple learn by eating the fruit of the tree of the knowledge of good and evil?*

  *If they knew good before, does it mean that the only thing they learned was evil?*

- Review "The Life of Faith: The Marks of Salvation" (pp. 36–37). Explore the effects of sin and what salvation and redemption do. Sometimes the marks of the wounds—inflicted on others by our sin against others, or their sin against us—are erased (as in Isaiah 1:18), but sometimes they are not (as in the resurrected body of Jesus). Ask:

  *Even though we want our wounds to be erased, why is erasure not always best?*

  *What does it mean to bear wounds that were once deadly and now are no longer so?*

- Review "The Church: The Community of the Redeemed" (pp. 37–38). Explore the implications of being part of a community that knows that sin is a reality and that God's forgiveness is immeasurably stronger.

  *What does it mean to you that God does not send us back to some place before the sin occurred, but forward from the place our sin spins us off to?*

  *What wounds stay with you as wounds of sin? How secure are you that those marks are drained of their deadliness?*

## Conclusion

God walks with the first people in today's story. Imagine God walking with you today. Think about what kind of relationship you have with God. Consider some ways that you might deepen that relationship and grow spiritually.

## Passing the Peace

The peace of Christ be with you.

> And also with you.

**Amen.**

# Sending, Gathering, Sending Again: The Heartbeat of the Mission of God

## Main Idea

Jesus Christ is present at the beginning of all things ("In the beginning was the Word"), and will be present at the end of all things ("In my Father's house there are many mansions . . . I go to prepare a place for you . . ."). All along the great arc from the Garden of Eden to the new Jerusalem we find Jesus Christ meeting us.

## Preparing to Lead

- Read and reflect on chapter 6, "Sending, Gathering, Sending Again: The Heartbeat of the Mission of God."
- Review this plan for the group gathering, and select questions and activities that you will use.
- What other questions, issues, or themes occur to you from your reflection?

## Gathering

- Provide name tags and pens as people arrive.
- Provide simple refreshments if other arrangements for refreshments have not been made. Review the ground rules and organization (for example, time to begin and end the gathering; location for meetings; welcoming of all points of view; confidentiality; and so on). Encourage participants to bring their study books and Bibles.
- Review the format for these gatherings: Gathering, Opening Worship, Conversation, and Conclusion.

## Opening Worship
**Prayer** (unison)

Jesus, you who are before, alongside, and ahead of us, we thank you for your presence with us. We claim the promise of your Holy Spirit, whom you send to teach us and to strengthen us to be vibrant agents of your mission. In our reading of Scripture and our conversation about life in you, help us to come to see your face and hear your voice ever more clearly, that we might follow you more nearly, and enjoy more fully the vibrant life for which you created us. Amen.

## Prayerful, Reflective Reading
- Read John 14:1–7, 25–31 aloud.
- Invite all to reflect for a few minutes in silence.
- After reflection time, invite all to listen for a word or phrase as the passage is read again and to reflect on that word or phrase in silence.
- Read the passage a third time, asking all to offer a silent prayer following the reading.
- Invite volunteers to share the word or phrase that spoke most deeply to them.

## Prayer
Loving God, hear our prayers today as we seek to follow you more faithfully:

(*spoken prayers may be offered*)

Hear us now as we pray together, saying, Our Father . . .

## Conversation
- Introduce chapter 6, "Sending, Gathering, Sending Again: The Heartbeat of the Mission of God" (pp. 41–46). Share observations, reflections, and insights.
- Review the Introduction (pp. 41–42). Share these key points:
  a. The great arc of God's mission is personal, not mechanical, not simply a matter of brute and mindless forces spinning along.
  b. Scripture reveals Jesus' presence at the beginning of the great arc of God's mission, and at the end.

- Review "A Basic Theme: Jesus Christ, the Face of God with Us" (pp. 42–43). Suggest that Christian funerals are one place where we are pointed to God's personal presence: Jesus Christ, who awaits us at the end of all things also meets us at the end of life. The church knows the person whose presence meets us in past, present, and future: Jesus Christ. Living along the arc, between beginning and end, the church lives in a regular rhythm of sending forth, gathering in, and sending forth again.
- Invite the participants to compare the verses in John 1:1–16 and John 14:1–7, 25–31. What common themes and promises are present? Next, examine the John passages with passages considered in earlier chapters—particularly Genesis 1–2 and Revelation 21–22. What themes recur? What is the significance of these themes and promises for your life?
- Review "The One Who Is There" (pp. 44–45). Jesus Christ is not simply out on the cosmic arc: Jesus Christ is close to us along the arc of our life, and the lives of those around us.

  *At what points in your life has the presence of Jesus Christ become clear?*

  *In what places or relationships has the presence of Jesus Christ been evident?*

  *In what ways does gathered worship help us become present to the God who is always present to us?*

- Review "The Church: Sending, Gathering, Sending Again" (pp. 45–46). Reflect on the pattern of the church's life, the deep connection between God sending us forth in the power of the Holy Spirit, and God gathering us in by the power of the Holy Spirit. Affirm that God is always seeking to bring us and others into communion with God and with others. Ask:

  *How does your own life of faith embody sending and gathering and re-sending?*

*In what sense is your sending, gathering, re-sending part of your congregation's life of sending and gathering? Of the universal church's life of sending and gathering?*

## Conclusion
One of the truths of Christianity is the constant presence of God with God's people. We are never left alone, from beginning to end. We are chosen, called, loved, and cherished. Name ways this truth informs our daily life and reassures us in stressful times. Offer a prayer of thanksgiving.

## Passing the Peace
The peace of Christ be with you.
    And also with you.
**Amen.**

# Want to Know More?

T. Desmond Alexander, *From Eden to the New Jerusalem: An Introduction to Biblical Theology* (Grand Rapids, MI: Kregel Academic, 2008). This book pays attention to the Temples/Tabernacles as the place of God's presence on earth, noting how strongly they are connected to the Garden of Eden and the garden city, the new Jerusalem.

Carol A. Newsom, "The Moral Sense of Nature: Ethics in the Light of God's Speech to Job," *The Princeton Seminary Bulletin* XV, 1 (New Series 1994), 9–17. Available at http://journals.ptsem.edu/id/PSB1994151/dmd005. This article focuses on God's speeches to Job, and how they frame the questions raised by Job's suffering, by his response to it, and by the friends who come to be with him.

Kevin Park, "The Nations Will Bring Their Glory" at https://perspectivesjournal.org/blog/2004/11/16/nations-will-bring-their-glory/. This homily has been incorporated into Kevin Park, *The Nations Will Bring Their Glory*, Theological Conversations 4 (Louisville, KY: Office of Theology & Worship, 2015). Kevin Park offers a striking, powerful reflection on what it means for the nations to bring their glory into the new Jerusalem.

Claus Westermann, *Genesis 1–11*, trans. by John J. Scullion, S.J., Continental Commentary (Minneapolis: Fortress Press, 1994). Westermann's commentary is thick and dense, a scholarly commentary in the best way. It is richly insightful for the life of faith, repaying what effort may be involved in reading it.

CPSIA information can be obtained
at www.ICGtesting.com
Printed in the USA
FSHW022107240519
58404FS

9 781571 532374